THE STORY OF THE
CHICAGO

CREATIVE EDUCATION

Published by Creative Education
123 South Broad Street
Mankato, Minnesota 56001
Creative Education is an imprint of The Creative Company.

DESIGN AND PRODUCTION BY **EVANSDAY DESIGN**

PHOTOGRAPHS BY Getty Images (Issac Baldizon / NBAE, Andrew
D. Bernstein / NBAE, Jim Cummins / NBAE, Jonathan Daniel /
Allsport, Gary Dineen / NBAE, Brian Drake / Time Life Pictures,
Garrett W. Ellwood / NBAE, Jesse D. Garrabrant / NBAE, Andy
Hayt / NBAE, Fernando Median / NBAE, NBA Photo Library /
NBAE, Scott Olson, Wen Roberts / NBAE)

LIBRARY OF CONGRESS CATALOGING-IN-PUBLICATION DATA

LeBoutillier, Nate.
The story of the Chicago Bulls / by Nate LeBoutillier.
p. cm. — (The NBA—a history of hoops)
Includes index.
ISBN-13: 978-1-58341-402-6
1. Chicago Bulls (Basketball team)—History—
Juvenile literature. I. Title. II. Series.

GV885.52.C45L43 2006
796.323'64'0977311—dc22   2005051072

First edition

9 8 7 6 5 4 3 2 1

COVER PHOTO: *Luol Deng*

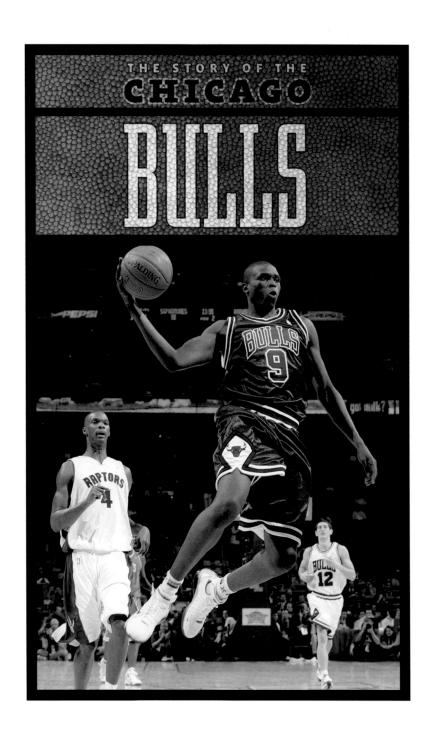

THE STORY OF THE
CHICAGO
BULLS

NATE LeBOUTILLIER

CREATIVE EDUCATION

Chicago was a stage.

HIS STAGE.

HE LEAPED OVER, DUCKED UNDER, AND DANCED AROUND THE COMPETITION TO PUT THE BALL IN THE BASKET. HE TWIRLED, JUKED, AND SOARED TO SINK IMPOSSIBLE SHOTS, OFTEN AT THE LAST SECOND TO WIN THE GAME. HE WORE BAGGY SHORTS AND STYLISH GYM SHOES, AND WHEN HE WAS CONCENTRATING HARDEST, HE STUCK OUT HIS TONGUE. HE WON TROPHIES AND AWARDS, CAPTURED HEARTS AND IMAGINATIONS, AND MADE HIS CITY THE BASKETBALL CAPITAL OF THE WORLD. MICHAEL "AIR" JORDAN WAS—AND WILL FOREVER BE—THE FACE OF THE CHICAGO BULLS.

CHICAGO BULLS
Chicago Illinois

SHARPENING THEIR HORNS

CHICAGO, ILLINOIS, WAS FOUNDED IN THE 1830S AND grew rapidly to become the United States' center for grain and livestock trade. Situated on the western shores of Lake Michigan, Chicago is known as the "Windy City," since its streets and buildings are constantly buffeted by strong gusts that howl in off the lake.

9

Norm Van Lier used his speed to spark Chicago's offense from the point guard position in the 1970s

One of the NBA's feistiest players, Jerry Sloan gave the Bulls 10 seasons of toughness and steady scoring

The people of Chicago are fiercely proud of their city, and it shows in the way they support their professional sports teams. In 1966, Chicago was granted a franchise in the National Basketball Association (NBA). Given the city's long history as a cattle town, coming up with a team name was easy. The franchise was called the Chicago Bulls, a name that symbolizes strength, size, and a powerful will.

Most expansion teams have a hard time winning games. But the 1966–67 Chicago Bulls were a pleasant surprise. Head coach Johnny "Red" Kerr put together a solid club that won 33 games in its first year—an NBA record for an expansion team.

From 1968–69 through 1975–76, the Bulls won 50 or more games four times and made the playoffs six times. Unfortunately, they were never quite good enough to make it to the top. Still, these teams were tough and gritty. By 1972, the Bulls had built a starting lineup that included combative guard Jerry Sloan, scrappy point guard Norm Van Lier, and hulking 7-foot center Tom Boerwinkle. The offensive punch came from forwards Chet Walker

JOHNNY "RED" KERR Johnny Kerr, or "Red," as most people called him due to his flaming red hair, grew up in the Windy City and was a basketball star at Chicago's Tilden Tech high. He went on to play at the University of Illinois and starred as a pro in the 1950s and '60s for the Syracuse Nationals, Philadelphia 76ers, and Baltimore Braves. But he came back home to Chicago to become the first coach in Bulls history in 1966–67, earning Coach of the Year honors that season. His coaching career did not last long, but he stayed in the game as a Bulls television broadcaster, a role he has played for 30 years. Bulls fans have come to appreciate his joking style and unrivaled knowledge of Bulls basketball.

and Bob Love. "Playing the Bulls is like running through a barbed wire fence," said Los Angeles Lakers guard Gail Goodrich. "You may win the game, but they're gonna put lumps on you."

During the late 1970s and early '80s, the Bulls faded in the standings. The Chicago franchise was left in disarray as it hired and fired seven different coaches in as many seasons. Prior to the 1976–77 season, Chicago acquired 7-foot-2 center Artis Gilmore, a player known as the "A-Train" because of his enormous size and strength.

Gilmore put up impressive numbers during six seasons with the Bulls, but a championship eluded him and the team. After the 1981–82 season, the Bulls decided to rebuild with younger players, and Gilmore was traded to San Antonio. "It's a shame we couldn't put a better team around Artis," noted Van Lier. "He did everything he could, but when we lost, he always got the blame."

BOB LOVE'S STRUGGLE

Stuttering can be a big problem. For Bob Love, it used to mean the difference between silence and speech. Love led the Bulls in scoring for seven straight seasons in the 1970s, and the franchise even honored him by hanging his number 10 from the rafters of Chicago Stadium when he retired. Love was smooth on the court but dragged down by an embarrassing stuttering problem off the court. "Butterbean," as he was known growing up in Louisiana, would get so flustered when he tried to talk that he often chose to be silent to avoid ridicule. Finally, at age 45, he decided to conquer his problem, attacking it the same way he got so good at basketball: practice. Today, he is a motivational speaker who speaks eloquently in front of large crowds.

BULLS

The "A-Train" Artis Gilmore earned a place in the Bulls' record books with 1,029 career blocked shots

13

THE SAVIOR ARRIVES

IN 1984, THE BULLS BEGAN A NEW ERA. COMING OFF a 27–55 season, they held the third overall pick in the NBA Draft. They needed help at every position, but when it came time to choose, the Bulls took a 6-foot-6 guard from the University of North Carolina named Michael Jordan.

Jordan had exceptional talent, but no one could have anticipated the shockwaves he would send through the NBA. With unstoppable moves, explosive quickness, and unrivaled leaping ability, Jordan soared to dizzying heights, averaging 28 points and nearly 6 assists a game as a rookie. Over the next few seasons, Jordan continued to sparkle, but Chicago remained an average team. The Bulls' front office knew that Jordan needed some help. When they picked up forwards Horace Grant and Scottie Pippen in the 1987 NBA Draft, the Bulls were ready to charge.

15

Arguably the greatest basketball player of all time, Michael Jordan could dominate games single-handedly

Coach Phil Jackson was known for his brilliant offensive strategies and ability to motivate his players

Behind Grant, Pippen, and Jordan, the Bulls became a powerhouse in the Eastern Conference. However, Chicago's quest for an NBA championship in the late '80s was consistently thwarted by the Detroit Pistons. The veteran Pistons slowed the Bulls by physically pounding the high-flying Pippen and Jordan. "They got in our head with the physical stuff," admitted Pippen. "But in doing it, the Pistons taught us the toughness we needed."

At the start of the 1990–91 season, the Bulls were confident that their time had come. Head coach Phil Jackson, who had arrived in Chicago a year earlier, had convinced the Bulls that although Jordan was their star, it would take major contributions from such supporting players as guard John Paxson and veteran center Bill Cartwright to win a title.

Chicago rolled through the regular season with a 61–21 record. In the play-offs, lying in wait was their old nemesis, the Detroit Pistons. This time the Bulls would not be intimidated, eliminating the Pistons in four straight games. Many of the Pistons' stars were so mad that they walked off the court in the final game before the last seconds had even ticked off the

SCOTTIE'S START

"Yo Scottie! Bring me a towel!" "Hey Scottie! Can you sweep the floor?" Scottie Pippen won six NBA championships with the Bulls. But for a while, it looked as though he might be more skilled putting a mop—rather than a basketball—in a bucket. In his teens, Pippen couldn't seem to get used to his fast-growing body and long, clumsy limbs. After high school, Central Arkansas University was one of the only schools that wanted him on their basketball team, and they gave him a scholarship to be the team manager in case he never got the hang of playing the game. Luckily for the Bulls, Pippen grew into his body and became a seven-time NBA All-Star, treating Chicagoans to a decade of the best basketball they'd ever seen.

clock. In the NBA Finals, Chicago faced the Los Angeles Lakers. The Lakers and star guard Magic Johnson surprised the Bulls in the first game, but the Bulls took the next four behind Jordan's strong play. After a 25-year wait, Chicago finally had its first NBA championship.

The wait would not be so long for the second title. The next season, the Bulls rumbled to a 67–15 record, breezed through the playoffs, and throttled the Portland Trail Blazers in the NBA Finals. The Bulls "three-peated" in 1993, beating the Phoenix Suns and star forward Charles Barkley in six games. Then Jordan, feeling he had nothing more to prove, decided to retire. At age 30, the NBA's best player walked away to pursue a career in professional baseball.

Horace Grant's clutch rebounding and shot blocking helped the Bulls capture three straight NBA titles

WINDY CITY'S SECOND WIND

THE BULLS WON MORE GAMES THAN THEY LOST THE next two seasons, but their horns were dulled without the presence of their superstar. Jordan, too, was a bit down and out. He was improving as a baseball player for the minor league Birmingham (Ala.) Barons, but his dream of making the major leagues looked dim. Even worse, his father, James, was murdered in a robbery in 1993.

In March 1995, after a year and a half away from basketball, Jordan returned. He elected to wear jersey number 45, since his usual number 23 had already been retired by the team. In the playoffs, Jordan and the Bulls fell to the Orlando Magic. Afterwards, Orlando guard Nick Anderson told reporters that the new Jordan wasn't equal to the old. "That number 45, he isn't Superman," Anderson said. "Number 23 was, but this guy isn't."

21

Dennis Rodman's superb rebounding was often overshadowed by his strange appearance and behavior

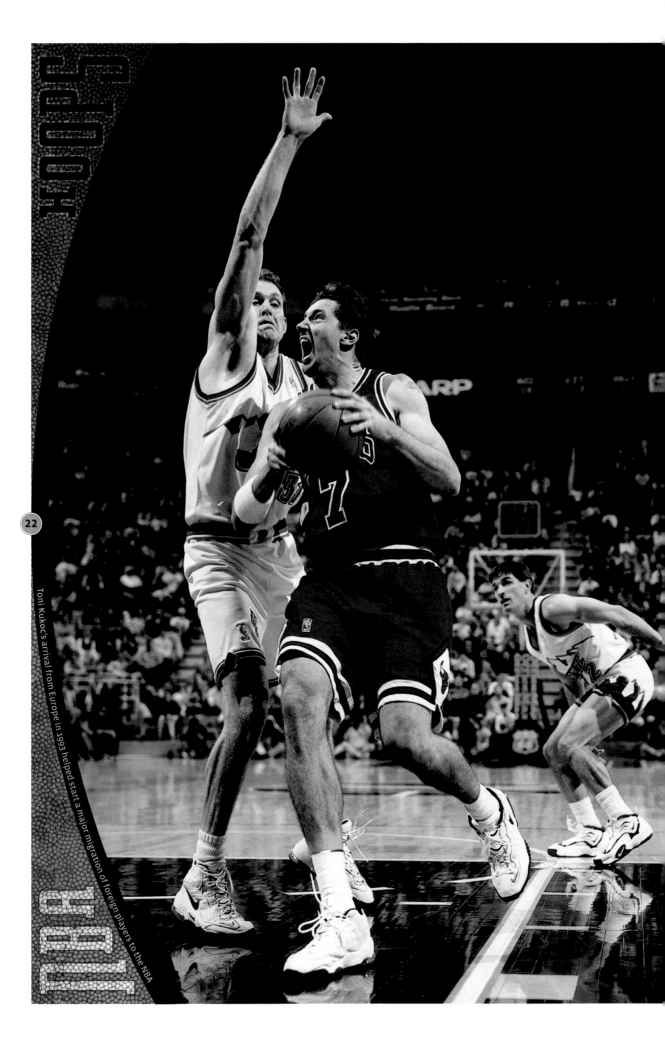

Toni Kukoc's arrival from Europe in 1993 helped start a major migration of foreign players to the NBA

The sting of the loss inspired Jordan, who went back to his old jersey number. The Bulls then added Dennis Rodman, a heavily tattooed forward known for his energetic rebounding skills, to the lineup. In 1995–96, Chicago's 72–10 regular-season mark set a new NBA record for most wins in a season. In the playoffs, the Bulls charged to their fourth championship in six years. "This means a lot to me," said an emotional Jordan. "People doubted us. We proved them wrong."

Over the next two seasons, no one doubted the Bulls as they stampeded to two more championships. Jackson's thoughtful coaching and a scrappy supporting cast that included center Luc Longley, guard Steve Kerr, and Croatian forward Toni Kukoc lifted the Bulls to new levels. In Game 6 of the 1998 NBA Finals—his final game in a Bulls uniform—Jordan poured in 45 points, including the game-winning basket, to top the Utah Jazz for the Bulls' sixth championship.

After a 12-year career in which he won five NBA Most Valuable Player (MVP) awards and rewrote the Bulls' record books, Jordan retired from the Bulls in 1998. Shortly after that, Pippen was traded away, Rodman departed as a free agent, and Coach Jackson left the team to join the Los Angeles Lakers. One of the greatest dynasties in NBA history had ended and was blowing away like dust in the wind.

Although often regarded as Michael Jordan's sidekick, Scottie Pippen was among the NBA's most versatile stars

UNITED CENTER RIMS

Throughout NBA history, teams have gone to great lengths to find a home-court advantage. Sacramento Kings fans clang cowbells to unnerve opposing players. The floor of the Celtics' old Boston Garden had so many hollow spots that the basketball often seemed flat. Denver's thin mountain air quickly tires out the Nuggets' opponents. The Milwaukee Bucks' tight nets let their big men get back on defense after a made basket. But Chicago's United Center, which opened for business in 1994, utilizes the advantage of... tight rims? The notoriously stiff rims have seemed to lower the shooting percentages of visiting teams for years, causing even the sharpest-shooting of Bulls legends, Michael Jordan, to comment, "It's just different to shoot here. I don't know if it's the rims or what; I can't figure it out."

THE BABY BULLS

LOOKING TO REBUILD, THE BULLS HIRED FORMER college coach Tim Floyd as their new head man before the 1998–99 season. But the Bulls struggled, setting franchise records for losing in Floyd's three and a half seasons as head coach. Their top pick in the 2002 NBA Draft, point guard Jay Williams, was injured in a motorcycle accident, and the Bulls made questionable trades and management decisions. Chicago became an unattractive place to play pro basketball. Even Michael Jordan spurned the Bulls in 2002, electing to play for the Washington Wizards instead in a two-year comeback stint.

27

A 7-foot-1 center with great quickness, Tyson Chandler was the second overall pick in the 2001 NBA Draft

Before going pro, Ben Gordon helped the University of Connecticut win the 2004 college national championship

Before the 2004–05 season, most experts predicted that the Bulls would continue to struggle. The Bulls started the season even worse than expected, losing their first nine games. But then something happened that Chicagoans hadn't seen in eight long years—the team started playing together...and winning!

Under new coach Scott Skiles—himself once a scrappy NBA point guard known for his heart and hustle—the Bulls turned their fortunes around. The Bulls started winning in streaks behind maturing stars such as guard Kirk Heinrich and big men Eddie Curry and Tyson Chandler, both of whom had been drafted straight out of high school and had taken longer than expected to learn the NBA ropes. Several talented rookies, including guard Ben Gordon and forward Luol Deng, also emerged as major contributors. "They are good," Coach Skiles said of his rookies. "You are never really sure what you are going to get even though they played big games in college."

For the first time since Michael Jordan left town, the "Baby Bulls" achieved a winning record and made the 2005 playoffs. They lost in the first round, but the Bulls continued their rise by returning to the playoffs in 2006. Chicago once again had a team it could hang its hat on.

The final image of Michael Jordan holding his follow-through as his title-winning shot went through the net in the 1998 NBA Finals in Utah was a romantic, lasting image. It will have to tide Bulls fans over until the next generation of Bulls can make some new championship memories for fans in the Windy City.

JAY WILLIAMS'S ACCIDENT

Ah, to be young and invincible. Twenty-two-year-old Jay Williams may have been thinking that very thing on the morning of June 19, 2003, just before he crashed his motorcycle into a Chicago light pole. Drafted by the Bulls with the second overall pick of the 2002 NBA Draft, the former Duke University standout played just one promising season before the crash left him with career-threatening leg and pelvis injuries. Still, Williams planned a comeback. In November 2004, he dunked a ball for the first time since the injury. "It was so exciting, I actually kind of cried," Williams said. "Maybe that sounds weird to some of you, but for someone who many thought wasn't going to be able to walk, to be able to dunk the ball is a great accomplishment to me."

Fans hoped that such versatile up-and-comers as forward Luol Deng would have the Bulls flying high again

INDEX